THE DOGFA

DOG WISDOM & LIFE

Whippet Edition

By Whippet Dog Gifts – Whippet Books

Alex „Dogfather" Luther

"As simple as walking a dog"

"Paw written Bible"

"Great gift for a dog lover"

TO KITE

INTRO

Greetings Whippet Lovers!

Welcome to „The Dogfather: Dog wisdom & Life lessons" – the paw written Bible every Whippet owner should have. The Whippet edition is here to provide with and also remind you of - those precious moments we spend with our four-legged friends - so many of them we take for granted and so many of them we just forget due to the hardships that life brings.

The book has more than hundred special dog wisdom sayings and cut-offs from life's moments experienced with Whippets. The intentionally designed dark theme of the book that resembles "The Godfather" movies, creates this „zen" environment and pictureless pages helps one focus better on the message itself in every page. Also, please do not rush and be sure to apply the message to your life with your Whippet as you flip through.

Editor's note

I really hope, that while flipping through this Whippet edition of „The Dogfather: Dog wisdom & Life lessons", you will be reminded of all the warm moments you had with your dog. Only after we loose our friend (and believe me – I know), we begin to cherish the small things and wonder how much another simple walk with our dog would mean to us.

On a happy note, please enjoy every page, let your thoughts flow and be sure to pet your Whippet after this.

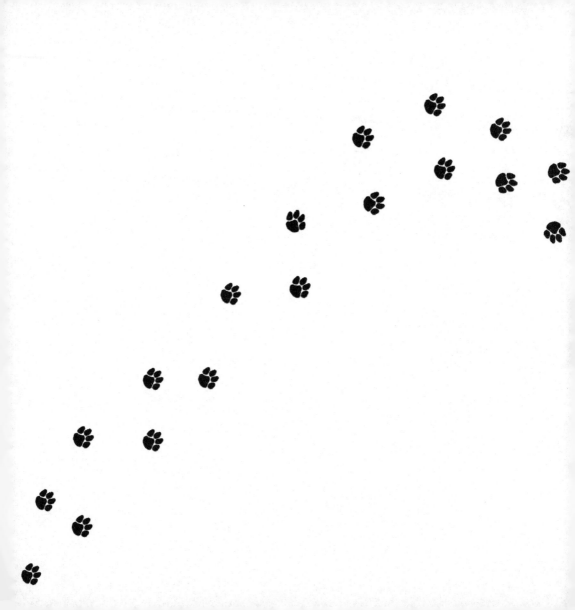

The Dogfather

"I grab her chin and look straight into her eyes. - Since the day I met you, you have done nothing but make my life better in every possible way. Do you understand?"

"*I think Whippets are the most amazing creatures; they give unconditional love. For me, they are the role model for being alive.*"

"There is no psychiatrist in the world like a Whippet licking your face."

The Dogfather

"When you feel lousy, Whippet therapy is indicated."

The Dogfather

"Whippets laugh, but they laugh with their tails."

"One reason a Whippet can be such a comfort when you're feeling blue is that he doesn't try to find out why."

The Dogfather

"Whippets are not our whole life, but they make our lives whole."

"a Whippet is living proof that God has a sense of humour."

The Dogfather

"Whippets act exactly the way we would act if we had no shame."

"*Heaven goes by favour. If it went by merit, you would stay out and your Whippet would go in.*"

"Happiness is a warm

Whippet."

The Dogfather

"Heaven's the place where all the Whippets you've ever loved come to greet you."

"Whippets are our link to paradise. They don't know evil or jealousy or discontent. To sit with a Whippet on a hillside on a glorious afternoon is to be back in Eden, where doing nothing was not boring—it was peace."

The Dogfather

"If there are no Whippets in Heaven, then when I die I want to go where they went."

The Dogfather

"You really have to be some kind of a creep for my Whippet to reject you."

The Dogfather

„*Whippets never bite me.*

Just humans."

The Dogfather

"Acquiring my Whippet may be the only time I got to choose a relative."

The Dogfather

"The greatest pleasure of owning a Whippet is that you may make a fool of yourself with him and not only will he not scold you, but he will make a fool of himself too."

The Dogfather

"If your Whippet doesn't like someone - you probably shouldn't, either."

The Dogfather

"I'm convinced that petting my Whippets is good luck."

The Dogfather

"Any man who does not like Whippets and want them about does not deserve to be in the White House."

The Dogfather

"One of the happiest sights in the world comes when a Whippet is reunited with a master he loves. You just haven't seen joy till you have seen that."

"The friendship of a Whippet is precious. It becomes even more so when one is so far removed from home... In him I find consolation and diversion...he is the one person to whom I can talk without the conversation coming back to war."

The Dogfather

"Buy a Whippet and your
money will buy love
unflinching."

The Dogfather

"The reason a Whippet has so many friends is that he wags his tail instead of his tongue."

The
Dogfather

"Even the tiniest Whippet is lionhearted, ready to do anything to defend his home, master and mistress."

The Dogfather

"The world would be a nicer place if everyone had the ability to love as unconditionally as our Whippets."

The Dogfather

"There's just something about Whippets that make you feel good. You come home, they're thrilled to see you. They're good for the ego."

The Dogfather

"The psychological and moral comfort of a presence at once humble and understanding— this is the greatest benefit that my Whippet has bestowed upon me."

The
Dogfather

"a Whippet can express more with his tail in minutes than his owner can express with his tongue in hours."

The Dogfather

"Love is the emotion that a woman feels always for a Whippet and sometimes for a man."

The
Dogfather

"I'm not alone, said my boy.

I've got a Whippet."

"Whoever said you can't buy happiness forgot little Whippets."

The Dogfather

"You can't have a pristine house with ten Whippets, and I'd rather have the ten Whippets."

The
Dogfather

"Sometimes I think I like Whippets more than I like humans. The only time a Whippet has ever betrayed me...was by dying."

"Whippets are often happier than men simply because the simplest things are the greatest things for them!"

The Dogfather

"*Investigators have discovered that Whippets can laugh, which can't be too big of a surprise.*"

"Our Whippets just need us and love, that's all."

The Dogfather

"Whippets are how people would be if the important stuff is all that mattered to us."

The Dogfather

"The more I see of the depressing stature of people, the more I admire my Whippets."

The Dogfather

"The greatest fear our Whippets know is the fear that you will not come back when you go out the door without them."

The Dogfather

"*Your Whippet might the only thing on earth that loves you more than he loves himself.*"

The Dogfather

"I love Whippets. They do nothing for political reasons."

The
Dogfather

"Hardly any animal can look as deeply disappointed as a Whippet to whom one says no."

The Dogfather

"Whippets are clearly the leaders of your planet. If aliens would see two life forms, one of them's making a poop, the other one's carrying it for him, who would you assume they assumed is in charge?"

The Dogfather

"You can usually tell that a person is good if he has a Whippet who loves him."

The Dogfather

"a Whippet's spirit dies hard."

The Dogfather

"Your Whippet doesn't care if you're rich or poor, smart or dumb. Give him your heart...and he'll give you his."

The Dogfather

"There is no faith which has never yet been broken, except that of your Whippet - in you."

"Whippets are my favourite people."

The Dogfather

"Our Whippets are grateful for what is, which I am finding to be the soundest kind of wisdom and very good theology."

The
Dogfather

"My Whippets have been the reason I have woken up every single day of my life with a smile on my face."

The Dogfather

"Whippets are actually very smart, it's just that they're rather clumsy, but it's this trait that makes humans attracted to them and why I love Whippets so much."

The Dogfather

"I have found that when you are deeply troubled, there are things you get from the silent devoted companionship of your Whippet that you can get from no other source."

The Dogfather

"When a happy Whippet licks your tears away, then tries to sit on your lap, it's hard to feel sad."

The Dogfather

"If I could be half the person my Whippet is, I'd be twice the human I am."

The Dogfather

"Did you know that there are over three hundred words for love in Whippet?"

The Dogfather

"When I needed a hand, I found a paw of a Whippet."

"a Whippet will teach you
unconditional love. If you can
have that in your life, things
won't be too bad."

The Dogfather

"Whippets have a way of finding the people who need them, and filling an emptiness we didn't ever know we had."

The Dogfather

"*Everyone thinks their Whippet is the best. And none of them are wrong.*"

"If you're lucky... a Whippet will come into your life, steal your heart and change everything!"

The Dogfather

"*Some people don't understand why my Whippet means so much to me. That's ok - my Whippet does.*"

The Dogfather

"The road to my heart is paved with paw prints of a Whippet."

The Dogfather

"The average Whippet is a nicer person than the average person."

Visit our store for great gifts for every breed

Etsy

Dogfather.us

Available at
amazon

The Dogfather

"Do you ever look at your Whippet and think... How did I get so lucky?"

The Dogfather

"A house is not a home

without a Whippet"

The Dogfather

"Stop telling me he's just a dog. My Whippet has more personality, integrity, empathy and loyalty than most people I know. He's family."

The Dogfather

"My Whippet does this amazing thing where he just exists and makes my whole life better because of it."

"You can always find hope in the eyes of a Whippet"

"Scratch a Whippet and you'll find a permanent job."

The Dogfather

"Wake up. Hug a Whippet.

Have a good day."

The
Dogfather

"Every Whippet must have his day."

"Anybody who doesn't know what soap tastes like never washed a Whippet."

"If all else fails – hug your Whippet."

The Dogfather

"My goal in life is to be as good of a person as my Whippet already think I am."

"My little Whippet

– a heartbeat at my feet."

"You may have many best friends, but your Whippet has only one."

The Dogfather

"If I had a dollar for every time my Whippet made me smile... I'd be a millionaire."

"Such short little lives our Whippets have to spend with us, and they spend most of it waiting for us to come home each day. "

The Dogfather

"If dogs could speak,

a Whippet would be a

blundering outspoken fellow. "

"Our Whippets have given us their absolute all. We are the center of their universe. We are the focus of their love and faith and trust. They serve us in return for scraps. It is without a doubt the best deal we have ever made."

The Dogfather

" It is amazing how much love and laughter they bring into our lives and even how much closer we become with each other because of them."

"When you think about it, what are the things that we most like in another human being? Many times those qualities are seen in our Whippets every single day - we're just so used to them, that we pay no attention."

"If we attributed at least some of our Whippet's qualities to a person we would say they are special."

The
Dogfather

"*After years of having a Whippet - you know him. Every twitch of the ears is a question or statement, every wag of the tail is an exclamation.*"

The Dogfather

Our Whippets leave paw prints on our lives and our souls, which are as unique as human fingerprints in every way."

The Dogfather

"Once you have had a wonderful Whippet, a life without one, is a life diminished."

The Dogfather

"*That right spot behind the ear, is where Whippets keep their souls.*"

The Dogfather

"Perhaps one central reason for loving Whippets is that they take us away from this obsession with ourselves. "

"I hope one day to react to something with as much pure ecstasy as I see in my Whippet's face every time I throw the ball."

The Dogfather

"You can't have too much Whippet in a book."

„By their delight in being with us, the reliable sunniness of their disposition, the joy they bring to playtime, the curiosity with which they embrace each new experience, our Whippets can melt cynicism and sweeten the bitter heart."

"I have a little Whippet who likes to nap with me. He climbs on my body and puts his face in my neck. He is sweeter than soap. He is more wonderful than a diamond necklace, which can't even bark..."

The Dogfather

"My cats inspire me daily.

They inspire me to get another

Whippet!"

The Dogfather

„a Whippet is like a person—
he needs a job and a family to
be what he's meant to be."

"One of the very best thing about our Whippets is how they just know when you need them most, and they'll drop everything that they're doing to sit with you awhile."

The Dogfather

"I don't think twice about picking up my Whippet's poop, but if another dog's poop is next to it, I think, 'Eww, dog poop!'"

The Dogfather

"If you live with a Whippet, you'll never run out of things to write about."

"The relationship with my Whippet is so much more physical than a relationship with another person. You don't get to know a dog by asking how he's feeling or what he's thinking, but by observing him and getting to know his body language."

"After dinner, he would prowl the grounds, sniffing the grass to learn what creatures of field and forest had recently visited. The yard is Whippet's newspaper."

When I think about it, all of this time my Whippet just tried to love me more - asking for only a fraction of what it gave."

"Unlike us, our Whippets live every moment and die only once."

The Dogfather

"I felt bad for screaming at him... I squatted down and rubbed my Whippet's ears. He leaned into the ear rub and sighed.

We started over."

The Dogfather

"In our Whippets' world,

would we be their best friend?"

"I never met a Whippet lover I didn't like. Makes you wonder..."

The Dogfather

"A strong man next to you in bed is a comfort, but real security is a Whippet bitch on guard at the door."

The Dogfather

"Whippets are angels full of poop."

The Dogfather

„One thing I particularly admire in my Whippets is how they don't waste time being afraid of tomorrow.”

"Just like you. Your Whippet has its day. Some even bite."

"Looking into my Whippet's eyes when I get back from work, remind me of my kids' eyes and how they used to welcome me back.

– Those who teach the most about humanity, aren't always human."

The Dogfather

"We are the same. Who loves me will love my Whippet also."

"If there is a place in heaven for Whippets (and I trust there is or I won't go)..."

"At the end of a terrible day I look forward to nothing more than coming home and lying on the bed, under the covers, with a little Whippet."

The Dogfather

"The best cure for a stick up your bum is a Whippet to play fetch with."

The Dogfather

I want to learn to love people the way I love my Whippet - with pride and enthusiasm and a complete amnesia for faults. In short, to love others the way my dog loves me."

"When was the last time someone was so overjoyed to see you, so brimming with love and affection that they literally ran to greet you? My Whippet will do that for me – five, ten, twenty times a day."

The Dogfather

"What is on your Whippet's mind while you take him for a simple daily walk? I bet it's:

- What could be better than to sniff the wind and be in the company of those you love?"

"After I bring food home from the grocery store...My Whippet looks at me as if I'm the greatest hunter ever."

The Dogfather

"*I wish my Whippets understood:*

- We're going in five minutes."

The Dogfather

"My Whippet can't think that much about what he's doing, he just does what feels right."

The Dogfather

"Although they have the teeth to tear, it is by swish of tail and yearning eyes that they most easily get what they want."

The Dogfather

"What would the world be like without music or rivers or the green and tender grass? What would your world be like without Whippets?"

The Dogfather

"Angels do not enter a house where there is a Whippet."

The Dogfather

"And he had a dog, a nice Whippet. He couldn't be too evil or dangerous if he had such a great dog."

The Dogfather

"You can't replace one
Whippet with another
anymore than you can replace
one person with another, but
that's not to say you shouldn't
get more Whippets and people
in your life."

The Dogfather

"That's the thing about being a Whippet - you were born for fun. What else could there possibly be to life? Eating was a thrill. Pissing was a treat. Shitting was a joy. And licking your own balls? Bliss."

The Dogfather

"-LOVE IS-

How excited your Whippet gets

when you get home."

The Dogfather

"One of the greatest gifts we receive from Whippets is the tenderness they evoke in us. "

The
Dogfather

„The face of my Whippet feels

like home."

The Dogfather

"My Whippet winks at me sometimes and I always wink back in case it's some sort of code."

"You'll never walk alone,

because I'll always be with

you.

With love,

Your Whippet."

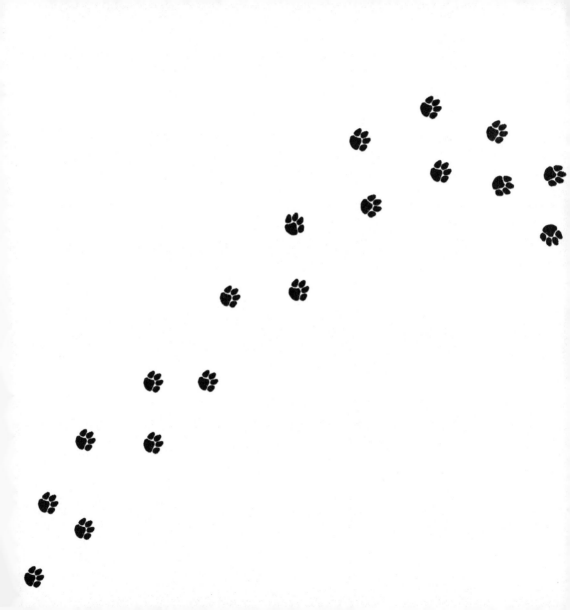

TO KITE

Final words

Thank you so much for taking a chance with the Whippet edition of „The Dogfather: Dog wisdom & Life lessons". Writing and editing this coffee table book was fun and relaxing at the same time. These simple quotes reminded me of how lucky I am to have a dog – a life companion. I really hope you've been reminded of the same.

Credits:

Janet Schnellman, James Thurber, George Graham, Mark Twain, James Thurber, Henry Ward, Bonnie Schacter, Edward Hoagland, Robert Louis, Robert Wagner, Rita Rudner, Stanley Leinwall, Daniel Pinkwater, Theodorus Gaza, Judy Desmond, Anne Tyler, Saint Basil, Caroline Knapp, Immanuel Kant, Franklin Jones, Groucho Marx, Joe Weinstein, Woodrow Wilson, Agatha Christie, June Carter Cash, Ashly Lorenzana, Jonah Goldberg, Dean Koontz, Clarence Day, George Carlin, Greg Curtis, Otto von Bismarck, Jodi Picoult, Ernest Thompson Seton, Gordon Korman, Doris Day, Roger A. Caras, Robert Benchley, Stanley Coren, Agnes Turnbull, Dwight Eisenhower, Dorothy Hinshaw, Sue Murphy, Alexander Pope, Ann Landers, W.R. Koehler.